SMETHWICK
IN OLD PHOTOGRAPHS

COLLECTED BY

JOHN MADDISON

Budding
BOOKS

A Budding Book

This book was first published in 1989 by
Sutton Publishing Limited

This edition first published in 2000 by
Budding Books, an imprint of
Sutton Publishing Limited · Phoenix Mill
Thrupp · Stroud · Gloucestershire · GL5 2BU

Reprinted in 2002

A catalogue record for this book is available from the British Library

ISBN 1 84015 155 2

Typesetting and origination by
Sutton Publishing Limited.
Printed and bound in Great Britain by
J.H. Haynes & Co. Ltd, Sparkford.

CONTENTS

THE SMETHWICK ENGINE was constructed in 1779 by Boulton & Watt to pump water up the locks at Smethwick on James Brindley's Birmingham Canal. It was housed in a pumping station at Bridge Street and was one of two engines originally required to supply water to the summit, the other being located at Spon Lane. The Smethwick engine was in use until 1891. It was removed in 1898, shortly after this photograph was taken, to the Birmingham Canal Navigation Company's depot at Ocker Hill, Tipton, for preservation. While at Ocker Hill it was seen by Henry Ford, who offered to purchase the engine and transport it to the United States. The canal company refused to sell but he was permitted to buy another Boulton & Watt engine which is now housed at the Ford Museum in Detroit. The Ocker Hill depot closed in 1959 and the engine was presented to Birmingham Museum of Science & Industry for display. It is now the oldest working steam engine in the world and can frequently be seen in operation. The site of the Bridge Street pumping station has recently been excavated.

INTRODUCTION

> In tracing the history of Smethwick, the first peculiarity which will arrest the
> mental consciousness of the observant reader will be the long continuance
> of the place in a state of quasi-oblivion.

This was how F.W. Hackwood, writing in 1896, summed up the early history of the
town. It is undeniably true that, prior to the advent of the Birmingham Canal and
the consequent growth of industry, Smethwick was a place of little significance.
The eighteenth-century village had no recognisable centre: its meagre population
was scattered, with the main areas of settlement strung out along the
Birmingham–Dudley turnpike road. At the time of the first census in 1801, its
inhabitants numbered little more than a thousand. Agriculture was the main
activity, although the traditional Black Country occupation of nailmaking was in
evidence on a small scale. Administrative affairs were governed by the Parish of
Harborne, of which Smethwick formed the northern part. The first church was not
built until 1732, its status being that of a chapel of ease to Harborne parish church.

The first section of James Brindley's Birmingham Canal, connecting the
coal-mining district around Wednesbury with the rapidly developing manufacturing centre of Birmingham, was opened in 1769. For Smethwick, the conse-
quences were to be far reaching: businesses, in their eagerness to expand, began
to look beyond the Birmingham boundary to the large areas of land adjacent to the
canal as suitable sites for new works. The first workshop to be built was the brass
foundry, from which Brasshouse Lane takes its name. It was in existence by 1790
on the site later occupied by the District Iron & Steel Works. Of greater significance
was the Soho Foundry, opened by James Watt in 1796 for the purpose of
manufacturing components for his steam engines. By the middle of the century
the largest employer in the town was the firm of Fox, Henderson & Co. which, in
1851, had the distinction of acting as contractor for the building of the Crystal
Palace as well as supplying much of the iron work used in the construction. Most of
the glass used was supplied by Chance Brothers & Co.; one of the few
undertakings in Smethwick not involved in the engineering or metal trades.

At the time of the Great Exhibition the town's population stood at over eight
thousand, but the most rapid growth was to occur during the latter part of the
century. A number of notable firms moved into the town during that period,
including The Birmingham Wagon Co. Ltd, Tangye Bros & Price, W. & T. Avery
Ltd which took over the Soho Foundry from James Watt & Co. in 1895, and
Nettlefold & Chamberlain. The latter company was later to amalgamate with Guest
Keen & Co., successor to the business originally established in Smethwick by
Arthur Keen, to form the GKN empire. The most striking feature of the town's
manufacturing output was its diversity; a characteristic which distinguished it from
most Black Country towns.

The rapid growth in population brought about an improvement in the status of
the 'insignificant hamlet': independence from Harborne was gained in 1856 with
the creation of a Local Board of Health. Under the chairmanship of Arthur Keen the
local board was responsible for many of the civic amenities and improvements

illustrated in this book. The local board became an urban district in 1894 and the town received its charter of incorporation as a municipal borough in 1899. Its status was further enhanced in 1907 when it became a county borough. By the 1920s, the town had grown to such an extent that it was having to look beyond its own boundaries for suitable land for housing. This resulted in a large area (not covered by the present book), including Warley Woods and Londonderry, being transferred to the borough from Oldbury UDC in 1928. Smethwick eventually lost its independence with the reorganisation of local government in the 1960s, becoming part of Warley County Borough in 1966. Eight years later, Warley was amalgamated with West Bromwich to form the Metropolitan borough of Sandwell.

To the casual observer, a town with so little claim to antiquity or architectural distinction might seem a poor subject for the photographer. That the area is well documented on film is largely due to the formation, as long ago as 1921, of Smethwick Photographic Society. Keen to record the changing urban and industrial landscape, the early members of the society came to an agreement with Smethwick Library for a photographic survey of the town to be carried out. The arrangement provided for the photographs to be deposited permanently with the library and it was through this that the pictorial civic record, from which many of the views in this book are taken, came into being. In pre-war days the survey was organised by Mr Sidney Smith who appears to have been the most enthusiastic contributor. Other members who produced significant numbers of prints were R.T. Newman, J. Edward Goodwin, Fred Parkes and George F. Greenfield. The latter was a photographer by profession who also undertook work for the Corporation on a commercial basis.

The survey continued after the war; with the creation of Warley and Sandwell, its scope was expanded to cover the larger local authority areas. The most prolific contributor in the post-war period was Mr Joe Russell whose work has appeared in a number of publications. In recent years, the society has established itself as one of the leading amateur photographic organisations in the country: it is host to an international exhibition, now in its fifteenth year, and has won the Minolta Photographic Alliance of Great Britain championship on seven out of the nine occasions on which it has been held.

Between 1954 and 1964 the Corporation produced a monthly bulletin entitled the *Smethwick Civic News*. Each edition contained photographs portraying the activities of Council departments and copies of the prints were subsequently deposited with Smethwick Library. Many of these were the work of Mr Frank Spiers of West Bromwich and a number are included here. Mention must also be made of Sandwell Council's own photographer, Mr Bob Binns, who, in addition to providing some of the more recent photographs included here, has frequently been called upon to exercise his skill in producing copies of old photographs for inclusion in the local collection.

Recent years have seen a growth of interest in the history of the town: Smethwick Local History Society was formed in 1984 and has become one of the most active historical societies in the West Midlands, while the creation of the Galton Valley canal heritage area has helped to foster an awareness of the town's industrial legacy. It is hoped that this book will stimulate further interest and provide a pictorial reference work for the local historian.

SECTION ONE

Streets

CAPE HILL developed as a shopping centre during the early years of the present century. It appears typically busy in this postcard view of 1938.

THE STRETCH OF HIGH STREET adjacent to Victoria Park was known as Bearwood Hill until around 1906. These two photographs were taken prior to the construction of the Council House and the electrification of the tramway. The lower view is from Coopers Lane, itself renamed Firs Lane in the 1950s.

THESE TWO PHOTOGRAPHS of the High Street were taken in July 1930. The lower view shows the end of the street and the junction with St Paul's Road (left) and Oldbury Road. The Empire cinema can be seen in the distance.

THE JUNCTION OF OLDBURY ROAD AND SPON LANE in 1927, showing the Spon Croft Cafe which stood on the site of the present public house.

OLDBURY ROAD, looking towards the junction with Spon Lane and Mallin Street, in July 1964. The road is now a dual carriageway, with a shopping precinct on the left and flats on the right.

BRASSHOUSE LANE, in November 1938. This view, taken from 'the steps', shows the District Iron & Steel Works on the right.

ROEBUCK LANE, looking across Galton Bridge towards West Bromwich, with Sandwell Park Colliery in the distance, in April 1925.

SIX WAYS was once regarded as the commercial hub of Smethwick but no trace of the district remains today. The upper photograph was taken from Windmill Lane in 1936, while the lower view, showing Soho Street, dates from 1928.

WATERLOO ROAD, from Bearwood Road, in 1931.

BEARWOOD ROAD, looking towards Newlands Green in 1928, showing cottages which were subsequently removed for road widening.

BEARWOOD ROAD in 1927, looking north from Hagley Road. The shops on the left were converted from houses in the early years of the century.

HAGLEY ROAD, looking towards Beech Lanes (now Hagley Road West) from the King's Head in 1927. The clock was later moved to the centre of Birmingham.

SECTION TWO

Industry

JACKSON'S FORGE which stood next to the Swan Inn, Oldbury Road, must have been one of the smallest workshops in Smethwick. The business originated in Low Town, Oldbury, where Charles Jackson became the proprietor in 1833, and was transferred to Smethwick in the 1850s. Described as a spade and shovel maker, Jackson specialized in producing tools for use in collieries and ironworks. The photograph was taken in May 1934.

THE SOHO FOUNDRY is probably the best known of all Smethwick's factories. It was opened in 1796 by James Watt for the manufacture of steam engine components. The upper view shows a group of employees of James Watt & Co in 1857, while the photograph below, taken at the foundry in 1919, shows a beam engine constructed by the company.

18

THE REMAINS OF THE GASOMETER, thought to have been used by William Murdock in his early experiments with gas lighting, could still be seen at Soho Foundry in 1921 (above). In 1895 the foundry was purchased by W. & T. Avery Ltd, a Birmingham firm of weighing machine manufacturers. Below is a view of the weighbridge department, taken in 1919.

THE DISTRICT IRON WORKS stood on the site of a brass foundry which was in existence by 1790. This view from the canal side dates from 1930.

GUEST, KEEN & NETTLEFOLDS LTD. main wood screw mill in January 1956. Three thousand machines were housed under one roof.

ALLEN EVERITT & SONS LTD. were one of the leading manufacturers of non-ferrous tubes. Originally founded in Birmingham in 1769, the firm moved in stages to the Kingston Works, Bridge Street, between the early 1890s and 1902. Both photographs were taken in 1924, the lower view showing brass casting using an electric furnace.

DIESEL-ELECTRIC LOCOMOTIVES standing alongside the Great Western Railway line at the works of the Birmingham Railway Carriage & Wagon Co. Ltd. in 1960, awaiting delivery to British Railways. The firm came to Smethwick in 1864 from Birmingham and became one of the largest employers in the town. By the turn of the century it had established itself as one of the leading manufacturers of railway rolling stock in the country, supplying equipment to many parts of the world. The works closed in 1963 and the Type 3 locomotives seen here were among the last items to be constructed. The 56-acre site is now occupied by the Middlemore Industrial Estate.

TANGYES LTD. was mainly concerned with hydraulic engineering. The firm moved from Birmingham in 1864 when the Cornwall Works were opened on the site of Rabone Hall. This view of the gas engine erecting shop dates from around 1909.

FLASH WELDING at the Halford Works of Henry Hope & Sons Ltd., metal window manufacturers, in 1954. The firm established itself in the northern part of the borough in 1905.

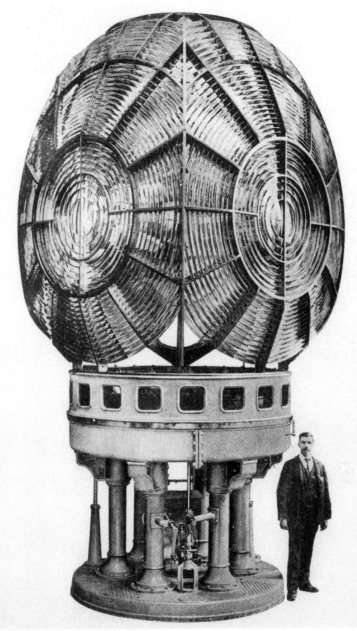

ROBERT LUCAS CHANCE acquired the British Crown Glass Company's works, to the west of Spon Lane, in 1822. Under his ownership the undertaking expanded rapidly. The manufacture of lighthouse lanterns, for which the firm was noted, began in the 1850s under the direction of James Timmins Chance.

PRIOR TO 1832, most of the glass produced in England had been crown glass. In that year, Chance's began manufacturing sheet glass using the skills of French and Belgian workers. This view shows the production of rolled plate glass by the automatic continuous process at the works of Chance Brothers Ltd., around 1955.

CAPE HILL BREWERY began operating in 1879 when Henry Mitchell transferred his operations from the Crown Inn, in Oldbury Road. In 1898 the business amalgamated with that of William Butler of the Crown Inn, Broad Street, Birmingham, and the firm of Mitchells & Butlers Ltd. came into being. These photographs from the 1950s show the No. 2 brewery (above), completed in 1912, and one of the high speed bottling plants (below).

THE WINDMILL, which gave Windmill Lane its name, was built in around 1803 by William Croxall. By the 1860s it had virtually fallen into disuse and, in 1886, it was incorporated into Edward Cheshire's Windmill Brewery, minus most of its machinery, and used as a storehouse. It was demolished in 1949, some 13 years after this photograph was taken. The brewery closed in 1914 and the buildings subsequently became part of Scribbans cake factory. They are seen (below) in 1960, shortly before demolition.

SMETHWICK'S ONLY COAL MINE was owned by the Sandwell Park Colliery Co. The first shaft was sunk in 1870 alongside the Great Western Railway line in the extreme north of the borough. Production ceased in 1914 but the engine house was still standing around 1956 when this photograph was taken. The lower photograph shows the company's coal wharf near the Summit Bridge in 1932.

WHEN CHANCE BROTHERS closed their stained-glass department in 1867 Thomas William Camm, in common with a number of other artists, established his own business in the town. He opened a small studio in a building in Brewery Street, but later moved to larger premises at the corner of High Street and Regent Street (opposite, top). The painting room is shown in the lower photograph with left to right: W.H. Camm, Iris Brookes, Eve Fell and Robert Camm at work. On this page is a general view of the studio. All three photographs were taken in 1930. The business was carried on by the Camm family until around 1963, but the studio has only recently been demolished.

THE TOWN'S LOCAL WEEKLY NEWSPAPER, the unusually named *Smethwick Telephone*, was founded in 1884 by the Ratepayers' Association as a means of making their views known. The original offices were in Rolfe Street and early editions were printed in Birmingham. From 1890 to 1908 it was produced at the premises in Regent Street shown above. A move was then made to a larger printing works in Hume Street, seen below in 1962.

Transport

THE MAIN ROAD THROUGH SMETHWICK became a turnpike in 1760. The toll house at the junction of High Street and Brasshouse Lane is thought to date from 1818, although there was a gate here by 1767. It is seen here in 1926, some 50 years after it ceased to be used for its original purpose. Now a listed building, it was used for many years as a ladies' hat shop.

JAMES BRINDLEY'S Birminham Canal was opened through Smethwick in 1769. Improvements were carried out by John Smeaton in 1790, involving the lowering of the summit, and it is part of this line which is shown above. The cottage was occupied by an employee at the nearby pumping station. Thomas Telford completed his improvements to the Birmingham Canal in 1829. A new line was cut through Smethwick (below), avoiding the locks on the earlier route. Both photographs were taken in 1932.

SUMMIT BRIDGE (above) was built in 1890, according to an inscription above the arch, to carry Roebuck Lane over the earlier canal. The same road crosses Telford's canal by means of the impressive Galton Bridge (below), which was constructed at the Horseley Iron Works, Tipton, in 1828/9. With a span of 154 ft, it was once the longest canal bridge in the world. Both photographs were taken in 1973.

A VIEW OF THE TWO CANALS from the site of the Theatre Royal in April 1957, showing Brindley's original locks and the aqueduct carrying the engine arm over Telford's canal.

THE JUNCTION of the old and new lines of the Birmingham Canal near Bridge Street. At this point the Thimblemill Brook passes beneath the canal by means of a syphon system. In this 1940 view the canal has been drained to enable workmen to locate a fracture in the syphon.

THE FIRST RAILWAY through Smethwick was the Birmingham, Wolverhampton & Stour Valley Railway, opened in 1852. LMS 4-6-0 No. 44764 is seen here passing the site of Soho station (closed in 1949) with a Birmingham–Heysham train on 8 June 1961.

WATCHING TRAINS from 'The Steps' – the footbridge linking Brasshouse Lane with High Street – in 1965. The foundations of the new bridge, built in conjunction with the electrification of the line, can be seen in the background.

THE STOURBRIDGE EXTENSION RAILWAY was opened in 1867, linking Smethwick with Old Hill and providing a through route between Birmingham and Stourbridge. A suburban diesel unit is shown leaving The Hawthorns Halt, opened in 1931 to serve the West Bromwich Albion football ground, on a Birmingham–Bewdley service in September 1961.

TRACK MAINTENANCE WORK at Smethwick Junction in June 1937.

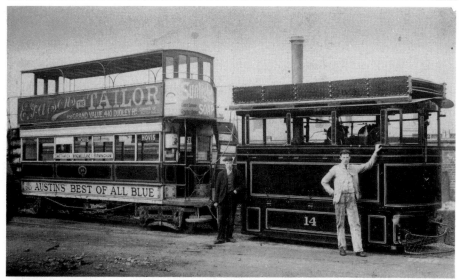

BIRMINGHAM & MIDLAND TRAMWAYS LTD. opened their steam tramway from Birmingham to Dudley via Smethwick in 1885. Engine No. 14 and trailer are shown in their later livery at the company's Oldbury Road depot.

BENJAMIN CROWTHER'S HORSE-DRAWN TRAM operated between West Bromwich and Smethwick from 1893 to 1903. One of the vehicles is seen here outside the Spon Croft Tavern in Spon Lane.

ELECTRIC TRAMS appeared on the Birmingham–Dudley route in 1904. Birmingham & Midland car No. 7 is shown here at St Paul's Road around 1908.

OLDBURY ROAD TRAM DEPOT in March 1939, just a few months before the tramway era came to an end.

THE LAST TRAM to run in Smethwick at the junction of Oldbury Road and St Paul's Road on 27 September 1939.

THE HAGLEY ROAD SERVICE between Birmingham and Bearwood was one of the first routes to be operated by the Birmingham & Midland Motor Omnibus Co. The Tilling-Stevens petrol-electric vehicle, shown above, was introduced in 1912. From 1914, the company's headquarters were at the Bearwood Road depot. The lower photograph shows the extension to the depot opened in 1936.

CHARLES SMITH, cab proprietor, of No. 394 High Street, in around 1910. The premises overlooked Victoria Park.

H. POWDERHILL'S LAST DAY on the cab stand opposite Rolfe Street station in January 1929. This was the last hackney carriage to operate in the town.

BRIDGES were usually tested by driving a pair of corporation steam-rollers across. The rebuilt bridge carrying Cranford Street over the Cape Arm canal was tested in this fashion in 1906.

MR GOSLING'S Wolseley two-seater of 1904 was reputedly the first motor car to be owned by a resident of Smethwick.

Houses

THIS GROUP of early nineteenth-century workmen's cottages originally stood at the approach to Soho Foundry. They are now listed buildings and lie within the factory gates. The dwelling nearest the camera, known as No. 13 Foundry Row, was the home of William Murdock for a number of years; a fact recorded by a plaque on the wall. The photograph dates from 1919.

RABONE HALL stood in a secluded spot to the north of the Birmingham Canal, with a drive leading to what later became Rabone Lane. A house had existed on the site since at least 1660. The earliest known occupant was Charles Lane, a member of an old established Smethwick family. Originally known as Smethwick Hall, it was renamed in the 1850s after the Rabone family, prominent Birmingham merchants, who had owned the estate since around 1780. The final owner was Joseph Gillott, a Birmingham steel pen manufacturer. In 1862 the house and grounds were bought by Tangye Bros. & Price who demolished the building and erected the Cornwall Works on the site.

SMETHWICK HALL, to the north of Stony Lane, is thought to have been built in 1746. It is seen here in 1904 when it was occupied by John A. Thompson. The Hall was demolished in 1937.

THE SPOUT HOUSE, in Taylors Lane, was also pulled down in 1937; the photograph was taken shortly before demolition. At one time it was a licensed house and known as the Spread Eagle Inn.

LIGHTWOODS HOUSE is thought to have been built in 1791 by a Leicestershire man named Jonathan Grundy. Throughout the second half of the nineteenth century it was occupied by the family of George Caleb Adkins, a Smethwick soap manufacturer. In 1902, largely through the efforts of A.M. Chance, the house and grounds were purchased by public subscription and placed in the care of Birmingham Corporation. The house is now used as a studio by a firm of stained-glass artists.

BELL HOUSE (right), seen here in 1936, stood at the junction of Bearwood Road and Waterloo Road. Its last occupant, Miss Sarah Hadley, bequeathed it to the Corporation along with the grounds which now form the Hadley Playing Fields. The house was demolished in 1959.

PAXTON HOUSE, in South Road, was once the home of Smethwick's first Mayor, Alderman Jabez Lones. The lamps were the result of a short-lived attempt to emulate the Scottish tradition of placing ornamental lamps outside the Provost's residence.

THE UPLANDS in Hales Lane was built in 1847 by Samuel Thompson, a member of a family of maltsters who came from West Bromwich. His son, Major Samuel Nock Thompson, presented the house to Smethwick Corporation in the 1930s. It was used as offices by the Public Health Department until demolition in 1958. The photograph was taken in 1939.

THOMPSON GARDENS, the first of several 15-storey blocks of flats in the town, was completed in 1961 on the site of The Uplands.

OLDBURY ROAD was raised to allow for the construction of the railway bridge in 1867, leaving these two groups of cottages, near Holly Lane, well below pavement level. Both photographs were taken in 1932.

BRIDGE STREET SQUARE was an early experiment in housing by the proprietors of the Crown Tube Works. The 28 homes were grouped around a central open space with gardens and trees. However, by the time this photograph was taken in 1932, it had become a slum and was demolished shortly after.

HOUSES IN PARKES STREET being renovated in 1934.

VICTORIA SQUARE, in Brasshouse Lane, was demolished in 1934, shortly after these photographs were taken.

CONDEMNED HOUSES which stood between the two canals, near Brasshouse Lane, in 1930.

THE SMALLEST HOUSE in Smethwick, No. 14 Oldbury Road (right), shortly before demolition in 1975. The width of the frontage was only 4 ft 10 ins, although the rear room measured a full 8 ft 6 ins across. It is likely that the two properties originally formed a single house.

RESIDENTS OF FOUNDRY LANE purchasing a mattress from the rag and bone man in July 1931.

WASHING DAY in Foundry Lane. These properties were condemned in 1934 under a slum clearance order.

BACK HOUSES in Baldwin Street revealed following demolition of the properties fronting the street during the redevelopment of the area in 1955.

AVERY ROAD, photographed in June 1981, shortly before the entire street was demolished.

THESE NON-PARLOUR TYPE HOUSES in Hales Lane were among the first council houses to be built in the Borough. The photograph was taken in 1927 from the corner of Mansion Crescent, looking towards Manor Road.

THE TRUSTEES of Dorothy Parkes sold most of the Old Chapel estate to the Corporation for housing in 1927. This terrace of four houses was built in that year.

BUNGALOWS for the elderly in Londonderry Lane, built in the late 1930s.

REDEVELOPMENT of the area around Windmill Lane began in the early 1950s. The top photograph opposite shows Redevelopment Site No. 1, looking towards Ballot Street and Windmill Lane, in December 1954. A later phase is shown in the lower view which dates from June 1962. The photograph on this page is of the French Walls Development in August 1964. Redevelopment of the area was not completed until the 1970s. Some of the earlier flats and maisonettes have recently been demolished.

A GYPSY ENCAMPMENT (above) on waste ground owned by the Birmingham Canal Navigations, at Roebuck Lane, in May 1935. Gypsies were frequently evicted from sites such as this. Cornelius Scarrat (left) avoided the problem by purchasing three houses at Bearwood. He continued to live in his caravan, however, which is seen here at No. 42 Gladys Road in September 1919. On his death in 1936 the caravan was burned in accordance with gypsy custom.

SECTION FIVE

Churches

SMETHWICK'S LARGEST CHURCH is Holy Trinity, built to serve the expanding central area, which was consecrated in 1838. It was almost entirely rebuilt between 1887 and 1889. A parish covering the northern half of Smethwick, known as the parish of North Harborne, was created in 1842.

THE OLD CHURCH, as it is now known, was the first church to be built in Smethwick. Consecrated in 1732, it was built as the result of a bequest made by Miss Dorothy Parkes. The exterior view dates from around 1901. The interior photograph, showing the east window, was taken prior to the removal of the organ to the west gallery.

THE CONSECRATION of St Stephen's Church, at the junction of Cambridge and Sydenham Roads, on 25 July 1902.

ST CHAD'S CHURCH CHOIR around 1903. The church stood on the corner of Shireland Road and Edith Road and was consecrated in 1901. It was demolished 70 years later and the site is now occupied by a filling station.

THE INTERIOR OF ST GREGORY'S RC CHURCH, showing the high altar. The church, in Three Shires Oak Road, was completed in 1934 and replaced the mission church which had been converted from a stable and coach-house in 1899. It was consecrated in 1961, two years after this photograph was taken.

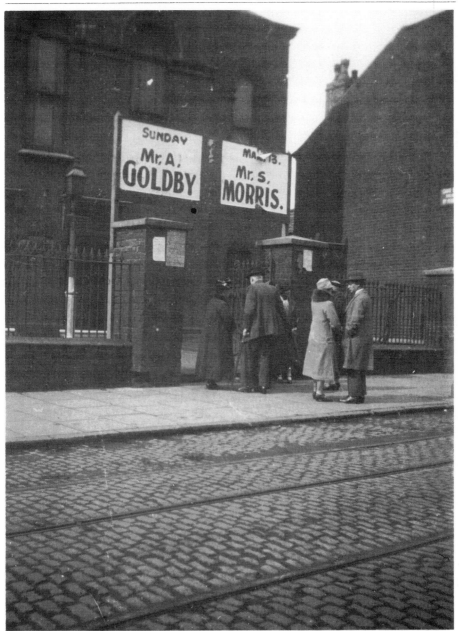

SPON LANE WESLEYAN CHAPEL was in the Smethwick circuit although it stood just over the boundary in West Bromwich. It is shown in April 1927, just prior to closure. The society amalgamated with West Smethwick when the new church at the corner of St Paul's Road and Holly Lane opened. The organ, which was built in 1799, was installed in the new church.

THE TIN TABERNACLE in Holly Lane was built in 1904. It was replaced by the present West Smethwick Methodist Church on the adjoining site in 1928 and used as a Sunday School before being dismantled in 1943.

THE AKRILL MEMORIAL CHURCH was completed in 1931 and replaced the chapel in New Street as the principal Methodist church in the town. It was built with funds bequeathed by Elizabeth Akrill of Edgbaston.

REGENT STREET BAPTIST CHURCH was built between 1877 and 1879. It replaced an earlier chapel in Cross Street. The congregation was formed in 1866 when the Midland Baptist Association sent an evangelist to Smethwick. At first he preached in the open, but services were later held in the mess-room at the Patent Nut & Bolt Company's works and in a shed in Union Street before the Cross Street chapel was built in 1866.

THE PRESENT BAPTIST CHURCH at Bearwood was opened on 25 September 1965, on a site adjoining the original 1903 chapel which is now used as a church hall.

CONGREGATIONALISTS came to Smethwick in 1810 when members of Carrs Lane church, in Birmingham, established a preaching room and Sunday school in the Cape Hill area. The High Street chapel, shown here in 1959, was opened in 1855 to replace a building on the corner of Crockett's Lane.

THE HIGH STREET CHAPEL was closed in 1961 and purchased by the Sikh community which had settled in the town during the 1950s. It was converted into a temple and became known as the Guru Nanak Gurdwara. These two views date from 1962 (above) and 1963.

THE SANDWELL GOSPEL HALL stood close to the canal in Brasshouse Lane and was used by the Plymouth Brethren between 1930 and 1969. It is seen here in 1953.

JAMAICANS attending their own service at the Temperance Hall, Bearwood Road, on 26 February 1956.

Public Services

SMETHWICK POST OFFICE STAFF around 1886. The first post office was opened in 1837 in a small house in the High Street. In 1890 a new head post office was opened in Rolfe Street. It remained until the present building in Trinity Street opened in 1968.

THE TOWN HALL, shown above in 1926, was built to the designs of Yeoville Thomason, a Birmingham architect, and opened in 1867. The building on the adjoining site (left) was erected in 1880 to house the free library, magistrates' court and offices of the gas undertaking. It became redundant following the transfer of the library to the old Town Hall and the opening of the law courts in Crocketts Lane, and was pulled down in 1931. The photograph was taken on 18 January of that year, the day before demolition work began.

SMETHWICK adopted the Public Libraries Acts in 1876. Space was provided in the Town Hall and the Smethwick Library & Literary Institute transferred its stock to the local authority. In 1880 a new library building was opened: the adult department is shown (right) in 1926. Reorganization of Council departments resulted in the library moving back into the Town Hall building in 1928. The lending library, in what was once the public hall, is seen below in 1955.

THE COUNCIL HOUSE was built to the designs of F.J. Gill, a Smethwick architect, as a replacement for the old Town Hall. It is seen (above) at the opening in June 1907 and (below) in 1935 with its Silver Jubilee decorations.

THE LAW COURTS, at the junction of Crockett's Lane and Paddock Road, at the opening by the Mayor, Alderman Sam Smith, on 30 October 1931.

THE FIRS CLINIC in Coopers Lane, shortly before it was opened in 1931.

A VOLUNTARY WORKER weighing a baby at an infant welfare session at Holly Lane Clinic in December 1959. The scales were made in Smethwick by W. & T. Avery Ltd.

HOME NURSES leaving the Edward Cheshire Nurses' Home in January 1957.

FUN IN THE SNOW at The Hollies Children's Home, Coopers Lane, in February 1955.

A VOLUNTEER FIRE BRIGADE was formed in the town in 1878. The manually-operated, horse-drawn fire engine seen above was housed at the rear of the public buildings. The lower picture shows a steam-operated appliance of 1904. Among those on the engine are Alderman Jabez Lones (seated, left) and Alderman George Bowden (standing, second from the left).

THE FIRE STATION in Rolfe Street was opened in 1910. In the top picture, taken in October 1931, a trio of fire engines are posed for the photographer in the station yard. The lower view shows a demonstration by the joint Smethwick & West Bromwich Fire Service at West Smethwick Park during the Festival of Britain celebrations in May 1951.

A HORSE AMBULANCE was given to the Fire Brigade in March 1894 by Smethwick Early Closers' Association. This vehicle remained in service until 1925.

THE AMBULANCE STATION in Londonderry Lane which opened in January 1961.

A GAS MAIN being laid in Bearwood Road, near Marlborough Road, in 1902. Under an Act of 1876 Smethwick Local Board established its own gas undertaking. The gasworks, in Rabone Lane, opened in 1881.

CONCRETE LAMP STANDARDS being installed in High Street, close to Holy Trinity Church, in June 1950. Electricity was first supplied to the town in 1898 by the Urban District Council from its generating station in Downing Street.

THE REFUSE DISPOSAL PLANT at Rolfe Street, under construction in May 1906. The destructor was brought into use in 1908 and operated for 40 years. A new plant, opened in 1956, incorporated the earlier building and chimney stack. The building of the destructor was first proposed in 1897, following the purchase of the Crown Forge site by the Urban District Council. It aroused much opposition among tradesmen in Rolfe Street, which was experiencing something of a revival at the time, following the blow dealt by the construction of the railway bridge and the consequent demolition of a number of properties in the 1880s.

Education

GIRLS at St Matthew's Church of England Primary School making baskets in May 1926. The school, in Windmill Lane, was built in 1861.

SMETHWICK'S FIRST SCHOOL was the Old Church School, endowed by Dorothy Parkes, which opened in 1734. The buildings on the corner of Church Road and Uplands, shown here in April 1927, date from 1855. The school closed in 1932.

HOLY TRINITY C. OF E. SCHOOLS were built in 1840/1. The buildings were photographed in 1939, around the time of closure. They were destroyed by enemy action in December 1940.

ST PHILIP'S RC PRIMARY SCHOOL was opened in Watt Street in 1860. The upper view shows the school to the right of the church, with the new buildings, which were to replace it, under construction. Both views date from 1964.

CAPE JUNIOR & INFANTS' SCHOOL, seen here under construction, was opened in 1888 as a board school for boys, girls and infants. It was enlarged in 1894 and 1901.

SPORTS DAY at Shireland Secondary Modern School for Girls in July 1960.

JAMES WATT TECHNICAL SCHOOL, formerly Smethwick Junior Technical School, took over the premises of Crockett's Lane Senior Boys' School in 1947. The buildings were originally opened as part of the Central Board Schools in 1885. This photograph, taken in February 1955, shows the removal of the tower.

HOLLY LODGE HIGH SCHOOL FOR GIRLS opened in 1922 at Holly Lodge (above), originally the home of the Downing family. A boys' school opened in the same building five years later but by 1932 both schools were housed in new buildings. The chemistry laboratory at the boys' school in 1961 is shown below.

DRIVING INSTRUCTION at Smethwick Hall Secondary Modern School for Boys in July 1963.

THE BRASS BAND at Uplands Secondary Modern School for Boys in 1962. The schools were opened in 1932 with secondary, junior and infants' departments.

A HOUSECRAFT LESSON in the unit kitchen at Sandwell Secondary School for Girls, Halford's Lane, in March 1958, shortly before the school was officially opened.

ENGINEERING STUDENTS in one of the machine shops at Chance Technical College in October 1960. The college had its origins in the evening classes organized by the School Board from 1885. The Technical School building, in Crockett's Lane, opened in 1910.

THE LIBRARY CORNER at Highfield School in 1960. This school for the educationally subnormal opened in 1959 to replace the Victoria Special School. It is now known as Arden School.

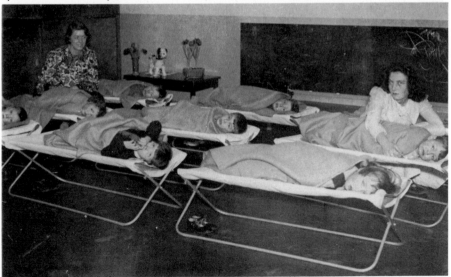

CHILDREN resting on their day-beds at the Edith Sands Nursery School, in Pottery Road, shortly after its opening in 1938.

THE SCHOOL CAMP at Ribbesford, near Bewdley, was given to the Borough by the Town Clerk, Mr Frank Chapman, and his wife. The top view shows a group of teachers in front of the main building, while below, attempts are made to produce hot water for tea. Both photographs were taken in 1928, the year the camp was opened.

SECTION EIGHT

Shops

FREDERICK & EMMA COLLEDGE outside their greengrocer's shop, on the corner of Baldwin Street and Cutler Street, around 1920. Frederick Colledge had previously kept a shop in Vittoria Street. By the late 1920s he was trading from premises in Oldbury Road.

PHILIP BILLINGHAM, boot dealer, stands in the doorway of his shop at No. 77 High Street around 1908. The firm celebrates its centenary in 1990 and is probably the oldest business now trading in the High Street. When the north side of the street was demolished in 1980 Mr Colin Billingham, grandson of the original proprietor, moved to premises on the opposite side of the road.

J.B. BLAKEMORE, seen here in the doorway of his High Street shop around 1900, was one of the town's leading chemists. The Smethwick & District Business Review of 1911 waxed lyrical over his 'capital consulting and operating rooms' where 'teeth are carefully and skilfully extracted ... by painless methods if desired'. The business was taken over by T.H. Martin around 1928.

FOR MANY YEARS, the corner site at the junction of High Street and Rolfe Street was known locally as Newbury's Corner. George Theodore Newbury, described as a linen draper, began trading here around 1870. The business was carried on until the early 1930s but, by 1933, the building had become a showroom for Samuel Smith & Sons Ltd. (opposite, upper), manufacturers of 'Foresight' grates, whose foundry stood close by in Brewery Street. Both the showroom and the foundry were damaged by bombing in December 1940. In 1962 W.S. Welch & Son, a firm of drapers established in the town since 1849, opened a showroom on the site (opposite, lower), adjoining their existing shop. This remained until 1974 when buildings on that side of the High Street were demolished to make way for the construction of Tollhouse Way.

THE PREMISES of John F. Meese, wine & spirit merchant, and W. George Ridgley, butcher, on the corner of High Street and Halford Street, in March 1934. Shortly after the photograph was taken, the shops were demolished and William Dallaway's fruit market (below) was erected on the site. Dallaway had previously traded from premises a few yards down the High Street on the other side of Halford Street.

WOOLWORTH'S High Street store in June 1961. Firkin's bakery was established in West Bromwich in the 1870s. Their branches are now a familiar sight throughout the Black Country.

THE MARKET, in Windmill Lane, in June 1956. This building has twice been gutted by fire and rebuilt: the first occasion was in 1928 and the second in November 1940, when the Luftwaffe scored a direct hit.

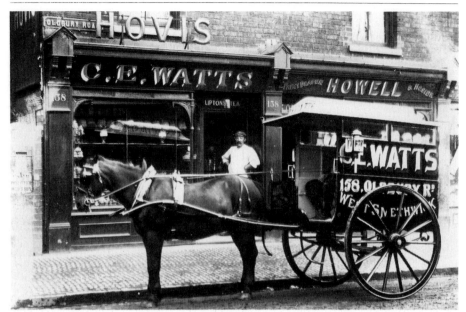

CHARLES ERNEST WATTS, described as a baker and confectioner, had two shops in Oldbury Road. His delivery vehicle is seen here in front of No. 158.

BOB MANSELL with a group of young cyclists outside his Oldbury Road shop around 1962. A keen cyclist himself, Bob started the business in 1958, but the shop fell victim to a road-widening scheme some 14 years later.

THE PROPRIETORS of the Victoria Fried Fish Saloon, in Watery Lane, clearing up after the floods of July 1927.

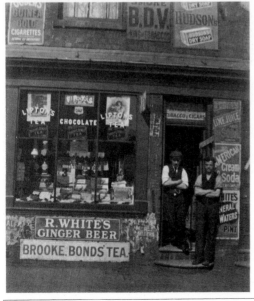

AN INTERESTING COLLECTION of enamel advertisements adorn the front of this small shop in Shireland Road, run by F. Watkins, in 1908.

JANUARY SALES at Tintern House ladies' outfitters, Waterloo Road, in 1949. The proprietor, Mr Christopher Stark, who started the business in 1922, is seen behind the counter in the lower photograph.

Public Houses

THE BEAR HOTEL at Bearwood is one of the earliest public houses in the area and was probably in existence by 1718. It has been rebuilt several times: this view shows it in 1902, some four years before its most recent reconstruction.

THE RED COW INN, demolished in the late 1930s, was one of the oldest buildings in the town, although the date 1587 inscribed beneath the window was fictitious. It was first mentioned in a deed of 1706. When the inn closed in 1937 the fireplace (below) was purchased by Alderman Sam Smith and installed in his home.

THE BLUE GATES was first mentioned as a licensed house in a document of 1781. It appears to have taken its name from the tollgates which crossed the turnpike road at this point. The building in the upper photograph, taken in July 1926, was the second on the site and was built around 1850. The present hotel, the dining room of which is shown below, was opened in 1932.

THE OLD CHAPEL INN around 1900.

THE WHITE SWAN INN was unusually situated between the two levels of the Birmingham Canal, near Brasshouse Lane. It is shown here in 1930, shortly before demolition.

CAPE HILL takes its name from the Cape of Good Hope Inn which stands at the foot of the hill, close to the boundary with Birmingham. The original house (above) stood next to a row of cottages and had an entrance at the rear in Grove Lane. The present building, shown below in 1930, was erected in 1925 as part of an improvement scheme which involved the demolition of the old toll house on the corner of Grove Lane and a number of other properties.

WHEN THIS PHOTOGRAPH WAS TAKEN around 1935 the old Spon Croft Tavern, in Oldbury Road, was being prepared for demolition. The much larger building which replaced it stands in the background, on the site formerly occupied by the Spon Croft Cafe.

THE GRAPES in Oldbury Road had the appearance of a typical Black Country beerhouse. George Stamp, the landlord, had been employed at Chance's glassworks before becoming a publican. The house was delicensed in the 1920s.

THE SWAN INN, at the junction of Oldbury Road and Holly Lane, is seen in December 1933, shortly before demolition. The new public house is visible at the rear of the premises. In the foreground is part of Jackson's forge.

THE KING'S HEAD, Hagley Road, before and after the rebuilding of 1903. The views date from 1898 and 1931 respectively.

SECTION TEN

Recreation

SKATING on the frozen boating lake in West Smethwick Park in February 1929. The park was given to the town by Sir James Timmins Chance in 1895. It was laid out on land which had previously been farmed by the Downing family. The pool was formed by the construction of a dam across the stream which forms the boundary with Oldbury.

VICTORIA PARK was laid out on the site of Pool Farm and opened in 1889. This 1955 view shows the main paths and flower beds.

THE LIGHTWOODS ESTATE was presented to Birmingham Corporation for use as a park in 1902. This photograph shows the reopening of the pool following alterations in May 1932.

HARRY MITCHELL PARK was given by Henry Mitchell in memory of his son, Harry, who died of typhoid in 1894. This view of the bandstand dates from 1930.

LEWISHAM PARK, seen here in 1962, was leased to the town by Viscount Lewisham and opened in 1905. The site had earlier been a football ground used by employees of the Birmingham Railway Carriage & Wagon Works.

SMETHWICK CRICKET CLUB 'A' team of 1887. The club was in existence as early as 1840.

SMETHWICK SHOOTING CLUB, photographed in Victoria Park around 1902.

THE SMETHWICK RECREATIVE & ATHLETIC ASSOCIATION water polo team with the Birmingham & District Water Polo League championship trophy in 1903.

SMETHWICK CORPORATION OFFICIALS football team of 1915.

THE FIRST PUBLIC BATHS, shown above in 1962, were built by the Board of Health in Rolfe Street and opened in 1888. The two pools were designated first and second class. This distinction had long since ceased to apply when this adult class (below) was photographed receiving instruction in May 1960.

SMETHWICK BATHS in Thimblemill Road were opened in 1933 and are among the largest in the Midlands: they have been host to international events on a number of occasions. The lower view, taken in 1956, shows the diving board and the stage which is used when the pool is converted into a public hall.

THE THEATRE ROYAL, in Rolfe Street, was opened on 20 September 1897 with a play entitled *Secrets of the Harem*. With a seating capacity of 1,700 it was one of the largest provincial theatres in the country. The first manager was Edward Hewitson, who was later to turn his attention to the cinematograph. Hewitson purchased the theatre after its closure in 1932, probably in order to prevent it being reopened in competition with his chain of cinemas. The building to the left of the picture, adjoining the theatre, was the scene of a serious fire in 1929 in which 11 people were killed.

THE RINK CINEMA, in Windmill Lane, opened in 1909 as a skating rink. It was converted into a cinema by Irving Bosco in 1912. The photograph was taken in May 1929, shortly before it was demolished to be replaced by the New Rink Cinema (below), later known as the Gaumont.

THE COLISEUM PICTURE HOUSE (above), in Bearwood Road, opened in 1911 despite consider-
able opposition to the granting of a cine licence. It was replaced by Edward Hewitson's
impressive Windsor Cinema (below), on the opposite corner of Dunsford Road, in 1930.
Little more than a year separates the two photographs.

SECTION ELEVEN

Rural Smethwick

PEGG'S FARMHOUSE stood on the north side of Cape Hill close to the site of the dispensary. The photograph was taken in 1898. By 1902 the buildings had gone and most of the land had been built over.

BUNCE'S FARM occupied a large area to the south-west of the High Street. The farmhouse stood close to the site of the present Devonshire Road and is shown here around 1905.

GREENFIELD FARM, in Hales Lane, was one of several in the area which was farmed by members of the Holloway family. It is seen here in June 1932.

ADKINS LANE, formerly Deer Lane, looking east towards Bearwood Road in March 1901.

THE LAST REMAINING PIECE OF MEADOW belonging to the Beakes estate, at Bearwood, photographed in 1930. The road in the background is Richmond Road.

OLD CHAPEL FARM, known in later years as Lowe's Farm, covered most of the estate which Dorothy Parkes bequeathed to the Old Church. The upper view dates from 1927 and shows the lane which led from the church to the farm. Below are the farm buildings and pool in 1925.

A FOOTPATH led across the farm lands from the Old Church to the Thimble Mill. It is shown (above) in 1927. The two felsite boulders in the lower view were deposited in the area during the Ice Age. They were photographed in 1930, by which time the trustees had sold the estate to the Corporation for housing.

LONDONDERRY LANE looking towards the junction with Manor Road in April 1928, shortly before the buildings on the right were demolished to allow the road to be widened. The boundary between Smethwick and Warley ran along the middle of the road at this point. A large portion of Warley was transferred from Oldbury UDC to Smethwick in 1928 and the area was rapidly developed for housing.

Smethwick at War

SMETHWICK VOLUNTEERS. The photograph was taken one week before the unit disbanded on 31 March 1908.

SMETHWICK SAVINGS WEEK 1917, showing the Mayor, Walter Henry Pollard JP and Borough Treasurer, Sidney Taylor, outside the Council House.

THE PEACE PROCESSION of 1919 passing along Waterloo Road, opposite Grange Road.

DEDICATION of the War Memorial by Revd W. Aylmer Rowlands, Mayor's Chaplain, on 18 April 1926.

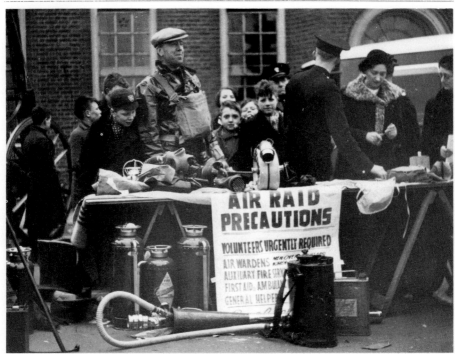

ENROLMENT of volunteers for ARP work outside the Blue Gates on 19 March 1938.

CHILDREN photographed wearing gas masks in Lightwoods Park in September 1939.

THE HOME GUARD parade at Cape Hill Brewery in 1940.

'DIG FOR VICTORY' exhibition held at Smethwick Baths in December 1940.

HOLY TRINITY SCHOOLS were destroyed by a land mine in December 1940. The remains are shown here in November 1946. Smethwick post office now stands on the site.

THE BIRMINGHAM CO-OPERATIVE SOCIETY BAKERY, in High Park Road, shored up following bomb damage in May 1941.

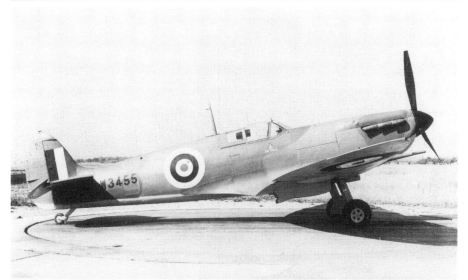

SPITFIRE No. W3455, presented by Smethwick Corporation.

ENTRANCES to two underground air raid shelters in Stanhope Road, near Church Road, on 16 June 1946.

SPECIAL CONSTABLES. The Cambridge Road section photographed in September 1945.

THANKSGIVING WEEK PROCESSION of 6 October 1945, passing the Council House.

SECTION THIRTEEN

People

CANON GEORGE ASTBURY was vicar of the Old Church for 41 years from 1884. Seen here at one of his celebrated garden parties in the grounds of the vicarage, he is the bearded gentleman behind the chair. In the centre of the photograph, making a speech, is Major Samuel Nock Thompson of the Uplands, while on the far right of the picture, holding his hat, is Edward Cheshire, owner of the Windmill Brewery.

ARTHUR KEEN was born in Cheshire in 1835. His early career as a railway goods clerk brought him to Smethwick where he established his own business and eventually became chairman of Guest, Keen & Nettlefolds. He has been described as the 'maker of modern Smethwick': in 1871 he became chairman of the Local Board of Health, a post he held for 18 years, and he presided over the town during a critical period in its municipal development. When, in 1888, a proposal was put before the Local Board that Smethwick become part of Birmingham, it was defeated by Arthur Keen exercising his casting vote as chairman. He died in 1915 at his home in Edgbaston.

HENRY MITCHELL was the founder of one of the largest breweries in the West Midlands. He took over the Crown Inn, Oldbury Road, from his father in 1861 and it was there that he developed a keen interest in the technical aspects of brewing which was to lead eventually to the building of Cape Hill Brewery. His son, Harry, died of typhoid fever in 1894 at the age of 32. As a memorial, Henry Mitchell gave 14 acres of land to the Borough, incorporating a park, cricket ground, drill hall and gymnasium. He was created the first Honorary Freeman of Smethwick in 1902.

JABEZ LONES was born just beyond the town boundary in Glover Street, West Bromwich. He began work at the age of eight at the Providence Ironworks, West Bromwich, and by 1874 he was the head of Lones, Vernon & Holden, the firm founded by his brothers which had earlier moved to Smethwick. Two years later he was elected a member of the Local Board of Health and after serving for a year as Chairman of the Urban District Council, he became the first mayor of Smethwick in 1899. He is seen here with Mrs Lones and is wearing the mayoral chain which he and his partner, Edward Holden, presented to the new Borough.

JABEZ VERNON was born in Smethwick in 1851. The son of Joseph Vernon, the town's first postmaster, he became chief moulder at the London Works of Fox, Henderson & Co. and in that capacity was responsible for supplying most of the cast iron pillars and girders used in the construction of the Crystal Palace in 1851. He died in 1906.

THOMAS WILLIAM CAMM was born in Spon Lane in 1839. He began working at Chance's glass works at the age of ten and, under the tutelage of Dr Sebastian Evans, became one of the principal stained-glass artists with the company. When the firm ceased producing stained-glass, he set up his own business in Smethwick. From his Regent Street studio he produced many fine window designs and examples of his art may be seen in buildings in many parts of the world. The business was carried on by members of his family for many years after his death in 1912.

A NATIVE of the Potteries, William Howson Taylor established the Birmingham Tile & Pottery Works, in Oldbury Road, in 1898. He specialized in fine art pottery, known from 1904 as Ruskin Pottery. This photograph of Taylor in his showroom was taken in March 1934, just over a year before the works closed.

RESIDENTS of Smethwick Hall relax in the grounds around the turn of the century.

GEORGE HUNT, aged 93, being presented with a silver tea service by Archibald Kenrick in recognition of 50 years service with Muntz's Metal Co. in November 1927.

OLD GENTLEMEN gossiping in Black Patch Park in 1932.

THE RT. HON. HAROLD WILSON, MP, Leader of the Opposition, speaking at Spon Lane Labour Club on 19 January 1964. In the centre of the picture is Patrick Gordon Walker, MP for Smethwick from 1945, who was to lose the seat at the subsequent general election. His successor was Alderman Peter Griffiths, seen below (left) with Borough Librarian, Kenneth Inskip, at an exhibition in March 1966.

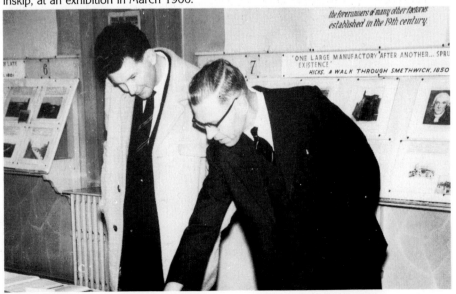

KEN WHARTON, of Hume Street, was well-known in the world of motor racing. He began driving in off-road trials in 1936 and gradually progressed to circuit racing, including a number of formula one events. In 1951 he won the Hill Climb Championship and he was also successful in long-distance sports car races. He was killed in a race in New Zealand in 1957.

SIDNEY SMITH was a prominent member of Smethwick Photographic Society in its early years. He was the organizer of the pictorial civic record undertaken jointly with Smethwick Library and personally contributed 876 prints and slides between 1927 and 1936, many of which appear in this book. This self-portrait was his final contribution.

Events

MAYPOLE DANCING in Victoria Park during the second May Festival organized by St Stephen's Church in 1903.

AFTERMATH of the fire at the Cornwall Works of Tangyes Ltd. on 4 January 1896. The view shows 'A' shop with the remains of the overhead travelling crane.

THE WORST FIRE to occur in Smethwick took place on 2 September 1939 at Rolfe Street, in the premises adjoining the Theatre Royal. There were 28 people resident in the building at the time and 11 of them lost their lives in the disaster. It was later established that a faulty electric cable was responsible for the blaze. The photograph shows the gutted remains of the building.

A PETROL TANKER crashed into Ansells Cider Stores on 24 April 1937, at the junction of Bearwood Road and Waterloo Road. In the fire which ensued the premises were completely destroyed but fortunately no one was injured.

ST PAUL'S CHURCH, after the fire of 3 February 1963. A new church, incorporating some of the remains of the old building, was consecrated in 1966.

THE WORST FLOODS ever recorded in the area occurred on 11 July 1927. Boats from the pool in Victoria Park were used to ferry people to safety from the vicinity of the Council House where a huge lake developed (above). Serious damage took place at Galton Junction (below) where part of the railway embankment was washed into the canal shortly after the passage of an express train.

SMETHWICK experienced another serious flood on 14 June 1931. Crowds of people gathered on the aqueduct in Stony Lane to watch the rising waters. The aqueduct, which carried a feeder canal, was replaced by an underground syphon system three years later.

ONE OF THE STREETS badly affected by the flooding was Rosefield Road. Residents are seen here clearing up after the 1927 flood.

RESIDENTS of Coopers Lane (now Firs Lane) attempting to clear flood water in July 1952.

A GROUP at the rear of the Blue Gates Inn on Diamond Jubilee Day, 1897.

ALTHOUGH the coronation of King Edward VII was postponed due to the King's ill health, celebrations in Smethwick went ahead as planned on 26 June 1902. The Mayor, Alderman Samuel Smith, is seen here in the procession passing Regent Street.

CROWDS AT THE CORONATION CELEBRATIONS on 26 June 1902.

THE PROCLAMATION of the accession of King George V was made from the steps of the Council House by the Mayor, Alderman William Henry Goodyear JP, on 10 May 1910.

RESIDENTS of Corser Street celebrating the coronation of King George VI on 12 May 1937.

POPE STREET, decorated to mark the coronation on 2 June 1953. The street was renowned for its displays and, on this occasion, was visited by several coach parties. Meanwhile, regulars at the Navigation Inn, Rolfe Street, joined in the loyal toast. At 86 years of age, Mr George Arm (centre) was Smethwick's oldest licensee.

THE CARNIVAL IN 1931 held in aid of local hospitals, ran from 20 to 26 September and was accompanied by a good deal of pageantry. The King of Mirth (left), Mr Claude Jephcott, was in attendance with his jester, Mr Frank Wincott, at the crowning of the Carnival Queen, Miss Evelyn Smith, seen below with her maids of honour and attendants.